I0471032

The Unconventional Road to Emotional Freedom and Prosperity

The How-to Guide for Today's Heart Inspired Entrepreneur

By Veronica Drake

Dedication

To my sons Matthew and Michael: you are my most prized accomplishment. I love more than my own breath. I am so proud of the men you have become.

Cover design: Bronson Dunbar, www.bronsondunbar.com

Photo of Veronica Drake: Terree Yeagle, Photographer
themomentphoto.com

To Holly Matson of Lightseeds: Thank you for polishing my
words. You are an amazing soul who just gives and gives.
www.LightseedsOffice.com

Copyright Veronica Drake, All Rights Reserved

September 2013

ISBN-13: 978-1492266068

The Unconventional Road to Emotional Freedom and Prosperity

The How-to Guide for Today's Heart Inspired Entrepreneur

Chapters

Preface

"The interval between the decay of the old and the formation and the establishment of the new, constitutes a period of transition which must always necessarily be one of uncertainty, confusion, error, and wild and fierce fanaticism."

John C. Calhoun, American Senator

Calling all Heart Inspired Women Entrepreneurs . . . Looking to create a stronger personal income and live life on your terms? This book is for you! I want to tell you right up front this is a business building book. It is NOT traditional and neither am I. To sum it all up - you CANNOT build your business or your life on "sand". This book is for the woman who desires to soar and to make change as she rises both personally and professionally.

Why did I write this book? Because I AM you . . . I WAS you . . . We are all one, and I am committed to sharing any experience I have had that can potentially help even one woman. Anyone who is drawn to me or this book WILL find its value and how to apply it to their lives and business.

Throughout this book you will see my vulnerability as I struggled through my "crap". My mission is to empower all the women who read this to become curious about themselves and ultimately dig deeper into how they can build a better life and business and create a stronger personal economy.

I have 20 years of self-development, business management and spiritual development under my belt. I have studied with some renowned teachers around the world and the ONE thing in life I am most passionate about is teaching women how to live out their dreams and be financially independent.

As business owners we cannot separate who we are and what we do. It is my greatest desire to help you develop the Soul of your business.

Foreword

'Get your head out of your ass!'

That's the very first piece of advice Veronica Drake ever gave me.

She didn't know me from Adam nor had we ever met, but that didn't stop her from telling me what I needed to hear – not what I wanted to hear.

No one had forewarned me of the dangers of following your heart. I quit my successful career of 12 years to listen to my inner whispers. God knows the whispering that was going on behind my back at that time: What an idiot for leaving to start a company in the beginning of a recession!?!'

People can be so (bleep)ing cruel. And, of course, I believed them. It's so easy to be 'positive' when things are going great, but getting out of that pathetic puddle was another story. I was broke from company start-up costs and scratching a living from side jobs when I heard about Veronica, or V, as I now call her, through my sister.

What I like most about Veronica is that she's been through the trenches herself in so many different aspects and survived. So, her advice is not only helpful, it's believable!

She also uses her intuitiveness about potential future opportunities which gave me back perhaps the most critical element, and that's hope.

Veronica reminded me that it's ridiculous to think of myself as a failure when I had not given my business enough time to grow, kind of like the story of The Fern and the Bamboo (look it up, print it out and read it daily!!!). She taught me how to attract opportunities and pay attention to the signs: 'What you want will unfold. But if you're looking for it only in the way you imagined the package being delivered, it will pass you by!'

Thank you, V, for being a truth teller in the most caring way possible.

I've always thought it's your killer combo.

Hugs, light and love.

Cynthia Lee Caruso
Caruso Media
San Antonio, Texas
www.caruso-media.com

Introduction

Overnight success took 20 years

Attempted suicide, divorce, infidelity, depression, 70K worth of debt to earning $7,200 in 4 days and being a sought-after business owner . . . that's my life over a 20 plus year span – yes, overnight success took 20 years for me!

My story began October 2, 1962. I am the product of an alcoholic parent and a bi-polar borderline schizophrenic parent. It was ingrained in me early on that women were second class citizens and they were the ones who ruined the economy in the '60's when they went to work. My father's line is, "Women don't go to college or even go to work - they marry men that have good jobs and they let the man provide for them." I remember always thinking that something didn't feel right with those words, nonetheless I gave them life. After all this was my only point of reference.

In 1982 I was 19 years old. I met my soon to be husband and instantly decided he was going to marry me, but first I wanted a baby. I talked him into it, and soon after was pregnant. Everything seemed perfect. We had a big wedding planned for March of 1983 and here it was November of 1982 and I was 4 months pregnant. I can remember thinking finally I was going to have someone in my life who would love me forever - the unborn baby. As I came to fully understand and embrace, all things are Divinely ordered and this baby was not meant to be born - I had a miscarriage. I was devastated.

Not only did I lose my child that day, I lost my hope of being loved forever.

I was more determined than ever to conceive again. Exactly nine months after I married, I gave birth to a baby boy. It was and still is the most exciting event I have ever experienced (the birth of both my sons will be the greatest accomplishment I will ever achieve).

My son had a rare disease that was not treatable by local doctors so he was hospitalized 60 miles away, and again I was separated from feelings of love and comfort. I was 21 years old, married, a mother, and suddenly caring for a sickly child.

I was giving a sick infant fifteen different kinds of medications and literally helping keep him alive. I barely knew how to keep me alive. Eventually he healed completely, and I learned a helluva lot that first year of his life.

Fast forward 3.5 years later – it's May 1987 and I am anxiously awaiting the birth of my second son. 1987 was a very pivotal year for me. Not only did I birth a son but I lost both grandfathers. My paternal grandfather passed in March and maternal grandfather in May. I was raised with my paternal grandfather, and literally thought I would lose my baby because I was so sickened by his death. While all that was going on I was separated from my husband who was involved with another woman.

I was raised on drama and it's what I thrived on. I could handle life when it was dramatic! My husband and I worked through it all, at least on the surface, and together we welcomed our second son into the world.

Fast forward to 1989 - I joined Weight Watchers and I lost a whopping 65 lbs. I had never in my life looked and felt so good. I was astounded, as was everyone around me. Suddenly I had more attention from men, and coupled with my underlying lack of self-worth, I entered into an extramarital affair.

The person I had the affair with was 17 years my senior, a heavy drinker, and physically and verbally abusive. This resonated with me. It was what I knew, and it provided me with the much sought-after drama I needed to feel alive. I stayed caught up in this self-destructive web of deceit and lies until I thought killing myself was the only way out.

In November of 1996, I set out to end the mess of a life I had created. I was careening my car toward a bridge abutment determined to end the suffering, all the while screaming nasty curse words at God. I asked Him why he let me have so much hurt my entire life. Why did he always abandon me when I needed him the most? As cliché as it sounds, while thrusting forward in my car suddenly I felt an incredible warmth come over me. It was like nothing I'd ever experienced. Simultaneously I felt an "energy" pull my foot off the gas and place it on the brake and I heard the words "I have always been here for you, ALWAYS."

I stopped my car and cried with all my might. I felt so many emotions in those few moments. I cried for the little lost girl who wanted a mommy and daddy to love her. I cried for the confused young bride who placed all her expectations on a good man only to lose her way even more and to ultimately break him apart. I cried for the misery I caused my family throughout the years, and I cried because I knew this was the moment I broke open and there was no going back. The only way to go was forward, completely exposed and vulnerable.

I had a serious one-on-one with God. I asked Him to help me put this affair business behind me and to help me heal myself and those I hurt. From that moment forward I began to see roadblocks in my way when I tried to continue the affair. It was like heaven and earth were conspiring to keep me safe and IT WORKED! With a lot of will power, determination and faith I became free!...now what?... NO DRAMA! I surely would have to figure out how to live without drama. And this is what I've learned, after I overcame and went on to birth a very successful business from nothing but a dream.

Because I was given the life I was given, I have been able to take all the amazing gifts wrapped up as adversities and write a story that supports my Purpose for being here.

I hope that you enjoy this book and more than that, I hope that you embrace the principles at a core level and really live your Purpose out loud, with a full willingness to experience what is.

Many Blessings,

V

Section One

#1 Align Your Inner Compass with Wealth

The secret to releasing self-sabotaging thoughts and attracting wealth.

"Not choice, but habit rules the unreflecting herd," William Wordsworth

What is a core belief? It is a belief or a set of beliefs you have learned from others in your life, either your family or society.

Just as a computer has an operating system like Windows, or Mac, we too have an operating system. The operating system (OS) is the first thing loaded onto the computer. Without the operating system, a computer is useless; it's the foundation for making it work. The OS is how it knows what it knows. The purpose of an operating system is to organize and control hardware and software so that the device it lives in behaves in a flexible but predictable way.

Much like that, our learned beliefs are our operating system. We go through life using that operating system. The problem arises when it no longer works for us and we begin to short circuit. When we operate from a series of learned beliefs, I call that operating on auto-pilot.

Our central processing unit is our brain. The brain is an amazing thing. I am by no means an expert on the brain, but I am the expert on me, and what I learned is that it's much easier for my brain to rely on what it knows rather than go out and create new.

Our learned beliefs create pathways in our brains. Instead of getting rid of them (which we can never really do), with intention, we can create parallel pathways that can bypass those old roads. Imagine a path in the field that is badly worn due to overuse; our brains are the same way. We think a learned thought and we travel the same path over and over and over. It is ONLY by making a conscious choice to become aware that we make change.

Any time you experience some kind of 'angst,' 'bother' or 'stress,' it is really a form of a <u>learned belief,</u> though we are never really taught to look at it as such. Notice where and how it feels in your body - tightness in the chest, or a spasm in your gut, or some other pain or discomfort.

The main culprit is actually fear; the stress response is a reaction to perceived danger, after all. However, our fears are often accompanied by sadness, frustration, anger, etc., and sometimes these other layers have to be dealt with before the fear can be addressed.

Your brain works the same way in forming how you think about yourself. As a child, your thoughts about yourself are formed from the messages you've heard and believed from important and influential people in your life.

For example: if you were continually made fun of by classmates and not invited to play with them, you have probably developed a low self-esteem thought pattern regarding friends and social situations. As an adult, obsessive thinking reflecting these patterns may automatically surface in social gatherings where you experience anxiety, fear and nervousness.

These beliefs are what we call your dominant thought pattern. They operate on automatic, like a habit, and are the thoughts that trigger, consciously or unconsciously, your feelings and reactions to the circumstances of your life.

Adopting Traditional Beliefs

Traditions are engrained in us at an early age. Day in and day out when we are growing up, we experience various beliefs from our families that leave an indelible mark on our lives. When you believe in a tradition, you must recognize that it has served some generation well; it had meaning and relevance. Yet it does not mean they are based in truth, nor necessarily have continued usefulness for your life.

There is a funny story about a woman who came from a family where the women always cut their roasts in half prior to roasting. The third generation daughter said she did it because she understood that it made the meat more tender. Her mother said that she learned it from her own mom and was told it was cut to reduce the cooking time and save on energy usage. When the oldest woman, grandma, was asked about it, she said that the oven she had when raising her family was very small and it was necessary to always cut the roast in half to fit it in!

So not only was there a belief being passed down that it was important to cut the roast in half, the reason behind the belief was totally lost and no longer relevant to the women's lives! This is a funny story and a harmless belief; of course there are much more serious consequences for some beliefs.

What Are You Tied To?

Elephants in captivity are trained at an early age not to roam. One leg of a baby elephant is tied with a rope to a wooden post planted in the ground.

The rope confines the baby elephant to an area determined by the length of the rope. Initially the baby elephant tries to break free from the rope, but the rope is too strong. The baby elephant "learns" that it can't break the rope.

When the elephant grows up and is strong, it could easily break the same rope. But because it learned that it couldn't break the rope when it was young, the adult elephant believes that it still can't break the rope, so it doesn't even try!

Humans operate in a similar way. We learned something about ourselves at an early age and still believe it as an adult. Even though it may not be true, we operate as if it is.

Fortunately, humans are born with the ability to make conscious choices - an important step in changing how you perceive yourself.

Good News For Us Humans: Thought Patterns Can Be Changed!

When you become aware of what you are thinking and feeling, you can choose and practice using new thoughts and behaviors. With practice, your new thoughts will become your dominant thoughts, replacing old patterns of thinking.

A simple exercise to illustrate how conditioned we are: Try lacing your fingers together. You habitually do it one way.

Now try doing it with the other thumb on top. Feels awkward, doesn't it? That's the valuable moment we call confusion, when we fuse the old with the new. CONFUSION IS KEY FOR CHANGE

Once confusion is introduced to the brain, the brain begins organizing the new inputcreating new synaptic connections (new pathways) if the process is repeated enough.

During the creation of that new habit, when conditioned or learned beliefs step in to protest you get resistance and we keep doing the same thing over and over again.

You cannot have a shift in belief unless you are willing and able to move through the unknown and go from curiosity to wonder. Rumi, the Persian poet, reminds us to "Sell your Cleverness and buy Bewilderment." Forget what you know and explore what's possible!

Now you have a basic understanding of one area where your belief systems come from. Let's explore how they might be keeping you "broke".

Being Wealthy: a Belief

It's time to shift your money mindset.

Consciously or unconsciously, we are also given a belief system about money. We all inherit a family legacy of how we view money. And, it is this very legacy that keeps generations in a poverty mentality and more often than not prevents them from having a higher level of income.

The emotional charge we have around money has very little to do with money itself, but rather with the underlying unmet emotional need. The belief systems you inherit are comfortable and give the illusion of safety, but in reality staying tied to a belief that no longer serves you is doing more harm than good.

Think about your money story. Take a few moments and reflect on what you heard about money when you were growing up. Can you hear your parents' voices telling you "there isn't enough"; "you have to work hard and the return is minimal"; or what about the phrase "**HARD EARNED DOLLARS**" – what effect does that have on your energy around money? Why is it when we hear the words "**EASY MONEY**" we automatically think something must be up? I'll tell you why; it's the way we were programmed to think about money.

Unconsciously this is how you live your entire life- not just your financial life. For example, if you were shown that there was never enough money and that no matter how conservative you were with it there would never be enough, you will inevitably live your life with the underlying theme being lack and control. As a result you might show up being overly controlling, a perfectionist and so on. There is a direct correlation between how you are with money and how you live your life.

How You Do Money Is At the Core of How You Do Everything - Especially Your Business

I really want you to think about this for a moment and consider how true this is.

- Consider your behavior patterns with regard to money, positive or negative.

- Consider how you feel emotionally and energetically when spending money, making money and saving money.

- Think about how it impacts your personal relationships with a spouse or business partner or your clients.

Right now I want you to think about your BIGGEST money issue. It could be that you're afraid to charge more in your business. It could be that you're in debt. It could be that you owe someone money or they owe you money. It could be financial issues in your marriage. It might be that you have no savings and you're afraid for your future.

My biggest money issue is: _____

Do you feel fear? Panic? What will people think? Do you feel an energy of contraction? Do you feel a twinge in your gut when you think about this money issue?

There is often a lot of "ewww" surrounding our money mindset and it's very real for women - and it is a MAJOR BLOCK. This is the primary reason why women business owners keep themselves below their financial potential. It's time to stop letting this HOLD YOU BACK.

How to Transform Your Mindset
Truth is, it isn't a lack of skill, capability or experience that holds most business owners back. It's their **emotional mindset.** The #1 secret to all success is developing what I like

to call a **D.I.V.A.** (Divinely Inspired, Victoriously Aligned) State Of Mind.

So what's a D.I.V.A. State of Mind?

It's the belief that **YOU are worth it** and **what you do is worth it** because of the power it has to transform the lives of your clients.

Creating a **D.I.V.A. State of Mind** is my favorite part of the whole business model, because of who it empowers you to *become*. No way you can hide out, play small, stay scared and doubt whether people will pay you what you're worth (and more) when you honor and truly embody the D.I.V.A. you are.

So how do you develop this D.I.V.A. State Of Mind?

First, you *DECIDE*. Then you **authentically uplevel in key areas of your life and business,** so that everything supports this awesome, empowered way of thinking. Here are 4 ways to start.

1. "DIVA-ize" your ENVIRONMENT.

Your environment will uplift you or pull you down and keep you stuck. What's your personal style? Do your office and home surroundings reflect your personal style? "Clutter" has a habit of creeping up and **clutter drains your energy.**

Your environment has a huge impact on your success and how you feel about yourself. Surrounding yourself with beauty doesn't have to be expensive. I create beauty weekly by going to the grocery store and buying a $10 bunch of flowers. The flowers make make me smile when I look at them. Just this little act of self-care will have a BIG impact on your bottom line.

2. "DIVA-ize" your SELF-TALK.

What are you telling yourself, day in and day out? Think back to thoughts, conditioned beliefs. Most women are playing a loop in their heads of criticizing, judging, comparing, and dreading who they are. Let's break the cycle!

Here's a simple, empowering action step to uncover some of the self-sabotaging messages you're not even noticing right now. For one day this week, have a notebook on your desk and just notice what goes on in your head throughout the day. No judgments, just observations –as a journalist would do.

Then notice – what are the key disempowering thoughts or phrases or beliefs that come up again and again? (Examples: "I can't afford it," "they won't pay for it" and any version of "not enough.") Pick ONE message to shift, starting right now. Don't you feel lighter already knowing you can do something about the thoughts?

3. "DIVA-ize" how you handle MONEY.

Here's the deal, D.I.V.A. – creating a business that pays you what you are worth means that greater amounts of money will be coming to you. How you handle that money will

---

absolutely have an influence on the clients you get and the fees you attract.

Cleaning up your "money clutter" can be overwhelming, so here's a simple place to start. Track EVERY bit of income that comes to you, every day, to the penny, and openly share gratitude for it. Your motto here is **"it all counts"** – including your partner's money. **ANYWHERE MONEY COMES FROM, BEGIN TRACKING IT** - a refund check, a dollar found in the street, birthday money, insurance reimbursement. Taking this stand of **"it all counts"** will help you begin to stop the discounting, separation and compartmentalizing that can sabotage your ability to attract and keep more.

4. "DIVA-ize" your spiritual practice

I have added to my spiritual practice the 5 R's - Realize... Reveal... Release... Reverence... Reciprocity. To help release residual resistance and experience the blessing of living from your Soul, practice the 5 R's daily. I've listed them out for you.

The first R is *Realization*. First you have to "know" that something is missing, off balance, not quite what it needs to be. You need to wake up to your life. So many times people walk around oblivious to what IS and they typically blame outside sources for their perceived "bad time." What are some signs that something isn't quite right? If you are experiencing any of these symptoms then it's time to open your eyes to what IS. Then you have to decide what steps to put in place to create your life.

- Cranky/short tempered
- Impatient/rushed
- Intolerant
- Tired/always feeling run down
- Overwhelmed and helpless

Here are some questions you can ask yourself to help create the awareness needed to realize what kind of life you are Really Living:

- Who do I surround myself with? Do they support the highest part of me?
- Am I kind?
- What do I do to nurture myself?
- What do I do to grow?
- What are my dreams?
- Have my dreams fulfilled?
- What do I stand for? What do I believe in?
- What am I willing to die for? Live for?
- What are my priorities? Are they different from what they should be, or are?
- What are my strengths?
- What are my weaknesses?
- What are my fears?

- What are my obstacles?

- What comes out of me when I am squeezed?

By contemplating on these questions, you will begin to become aware of negativity and begin the necessary work to rectify it. Self-analysis is key to realization.

Jump ahead 50 years and write the story of your life. Think out of the box. Define who you are, what traits and characteristics do you admire. Speak to your integrity and generosity. What contributions have you made to the world, what talents have you developed and shared over the years. Write the story you want told about you in 50 years. EGO plays no part in this exercise - this is an exercise to see who you are and who you will always be. Honesty and self-love will guide you as you write, I promise.

The second R is *Revelation*. Once you realize something is "off", it's time to uncover the truth about what's going on inside. Be willing to unpack the boxes. I liken the unpacking and storage of your "stuff" to old boxes we keep in our basements or attics. Stuff that truly no longer serves us but we can't seem to get rid of it. Whether we say we don't have the time, the energy or the desire, the boxes continue to pile up as we keep adding to them and never dispose of any.

Maybe it's the kids' old craft projects they made in 3rd grade and now they are 30 years old, or maybe it's clothes you wore in 1970 (4 sizes and 29 years ago), or maybe it's old resentments towards someone who "did you wrong", or bitterness toward a sibling or friend for not knowing better, or jealousy toward just about everyone in the world because obviously everyone has it better than you. You see what I mean about the boxes, yes?

What is it in your life that YOU need to reveal? Take time to journal your thoughts on relationships, past and present. Are you keeping any old "boxes" that aren't necessary?

As we learned above, to reveal means to face it and once you come face to face with it, it's time to RELEASE it.

The third R is Release. This is our next step; all are equally difficult but this perhaps this is the most difficult because there truly is no fooling yourself. Either you release it or you don't. You will know by reviewing the symptoms in Step One.

The Releasing process:

- Embrace your greatest good (why you came here)

  Define the greatest good in your reality: spiritually and energetically. There is a force constantly at work in the universe; energy connected to our greatest potential in any situation. What is YOUR greatest potential in this given situation? What Soul lesson do you need to experience at this moment in time? This "knowing" comes through your intuition. Keep your vision on your greatest good, found at a Soul Level.

- Explore perceptions

Become the "other person" and try on their version. Could there be another way to see a situation? What did they come here to learn from this interaction? Is the fact that your best friend was talking about you or is it REALLY the way YOU feel about the friend talking behind your back?

- Eliminate distractions

Simplify your thoughts. Gain clarity and grace by eliminating mind chatter. Practice meditation and connecting to Source.

- Engage your Soul

Tune in to your intuition (the quiet voice or subtle pang inside of you) and ask what you need to do to live Soul-fully at this given moment in time. Simply ask yourself: who would I be without this thought?

Often we need assistance with this process.

I am a huge advocate of psychotherapy. Some of my deepest revelations came after an intense session, not necessarily during a session. The therapist is like the archeologist. They excavate, exhume and help you find the buried tomb, the tomb that holds the key to your personal freedom. They can help you establish dates and timelines and reconnect memories if necessary. Make no mistake, they are simply there to assist you in the find - it is YOUR responsibility to take the find and make it your treasure.

The fourth R is Reverence. Reverence is to recognize and honor the presence of the sacred in everything. Being grateful is a way to show respect or honor to your higher power. Having an attitude of gratitude or "How may I serve?" supports reverence. Show appreciation for WHAT IS and accepting WHAT IS.

A way to show reverence is to set aside quiet time to commune with your higher power.

Your mind has many thoughts and it is nearly impossible to shut it all off. Do not be hard on yourself. Focusing on your breathing is a classic way to silence your mind; if a thought floats in simply ask it to leave and return to conscious breathing. Ask that a state of mental relaxation comes to you. If you are hard on yourself you completely defeat the purpose of this exercise. Love and honor exactly where you are; simply allow yourself the gift of acceptance. Release any negative thoughts through breath and take in thoughts of joy and kindness through the breath. When you practice stillness, you will begin enjoying communion with your Creator in the way only you can. Remember, there is no right or wrong way to have a relationship with Source.

This story comes from the Buddhist teachings and describes beautifully the stilling the mind.

It is said that a most intelligent man once came to the Zen Master Nannin seeking answers to the mystery of life. Being a professor of philosophy, the man's queries about God and meditation were endless. The master listened in silence.

When the man had temporarily exhausted his requests, the master said, "You look tired. Having climbed this high mountain and traveled to this faraway place, come and rest, while I prepare your tea."

Although his mind boiled with questions, the professor waited while the tea brewed. As its rich aroma filled the room the Master said, "Be patient. Don't be in such a hurry. Who knows? Even by drinking tea, your questions may be answered. "At this the professor began to doubt the wisdom of the teacher. He began wondering if his entire journey had been a waste of time. This man seems mad, he thought. What do my questions about God and the divine have to do with tea? Yet the professor was indeed tired, as the master had perceived, and if he was soon to descend this mount he needed refreshment.

The Master brought the kettle, poured the tea in the cup and the tea started overflowing into the saucer. The professor was startled by the clumsiness and amazed when the master continued to allow the tea to flow until the saucer also was filled. Just one more drop and the tea would start flowing onto the table and the floor.

The professor exclaimed, "Stop! What are you doing! Can't you see the cup is full and the saucer is full?"

Nannin replied, "That is the exact condition you find yourself in.

"Your mind is so full of questions that even if I answer, you don't have any space to receive the wisdom. Since you entered this palace, your questions have overflowed. This small abode is filled with your questions.

"Return from whence you came, empty your cup and then come. If you are to fulfill your desire to know the great mysteries of life, you must first create a space for them to enter."

Stilling your mind is essential for communion. It is very difficult to have communion, to have a conversation, whether it is with God or a friend, when there is no time of stilling your mind. For communion, there must be a time of receiving what the other has to give. Stilling the mind is essential to those seeking the revelation of God.

This is ultimately what we strive for when we practice meditation. This is WHY we meditate: Guidance. Wisdom.

We call ourselves human beings when in reality we are spiritual beings. You are a soul and your essence is spirit. You begin to know and live this truth as you reveal God in your consciousness and your life.

Meditation is the time and space you make daily for God in your life.

There are many purposes for meditation:

- Greater awareness of who you are and your purpose for existence.

- To be able to experience complete joy.

- To have a greater sense of caring about yourself and other people.

- To revitalize your mind, your body, and your spirit.

Your prayers are an integral part of your well-being. Every religion in the world has is a form of prayer that is taught. Prayer is the capacity to state what you desire. Meditation is the skilled stilling of the mind to receive an answer.

There is another story I'd like to share with you about prayer that I found, as a teacher, insightful, and perhaps you will derive inspiration as well.

It is said that one of the great spiritual Masters, Moses, once came upon a man who was praying. The man's prayer sounded so strange that Moses stopped.

As he listened, he realized the man's prayer was insulting to God. "Let me come close to you," the man prayed, "and I promise to clean your body when it is dirty. If lice are there, I will take them away. And I am a good shoemaker. I will make you perfect shoes.

"Nobody looks after your needs Lord. I will make sure your needs are met. If you fall ill, I will serve you and bring to you what will cleanse you of sickness. I know how to cook and I will prepare lavish feasts of nourishment for you."

Enraged, Moses interrupted the man shouting, "Stop! Stop! You heretic. What are you saying? That God has lice on his body? That God's clothes are dirty and that you will clean them? That God can be ill and have need for food that you will cook for him? Who taught you this prayer?"

Stunned, the man tearfully replied, "No one taught me this prayer. I have not learned it from anywhere. I am very poor and I am very uneducated and I don't know how to pray. I have made it up from the thing I know.

"Life troubles me very much, so it must trouble God. Sometimes the food I find is not very good and my stomach aches. God must also suffer in this way sometimes. This is just my own experience that has become my prayer, but if you know the right prayer please teach me."

Filled with compassion, Moses taught the man the right prayer. The man bowed down to Moses, thanking him as tears of deep gratitude flowed from his eyes. The man departed and Moses was very pleased

---

at this opportunity to help another to see his error and learn the correct way to pray.

While Moses slept, God appeared to him in a dream. His voice filled with anger, God said, "I sent you there to bring people closer to me but now you have thrown away one of my greatest lovers. This right prayer you have taught him will keep him from me. He will now only repeat the words you have told him.

"Those words will be a barrier between his spirit and mine. It is not a prayer at all.

"Prayer has nothing to do with law. Prayer is the love. Love is a law onto itself. It needs no other law.

"Know that, my servant, with love comes grace. With love comes truth. Truth is the liberation of the spirit."

Your prayers are important in meditation. Prayer is a very personal process and one that is never done incorrectly. What matters is that your prayer comes from your heart.

The fifth R is Reciprocity. The way to receive is to give. Be generous with your time, treasure and talent. Be mindful to take your gratitude to Spirit daily.

How you can build reciprocity:

- Give what you can - not necessarily dollars, but time and/or talents
- Volunteer
- Be a big brother/big sister
- Support a charity

- Start a Soul Circle group

- Support a cause

- Give time back to your creator.

- Create a "quiet space" to commune and bring your gratitude.

- Be mindful when you speak to Spirit that you are asking how you may serve.

- Be humble

The **Analects** of Confucius says:

"Exert yourself to achieve your proper merit. In giving heed to the beginning, think of the end. Then the end will be without distress. God will lead men to tranquil security. Seek to be in harmony with all your neighbors. Live in amenity with all your neighbors. Tranquilize and serve others."

Self-worth is directly tied to net worth.

How You Treat Yourself Has EVERYTHING to Do With Receiving Higher Fees

You can't attract clients who value you until you do the work and value yourself. Then your programs and services become powerful possibilities for your clients to step INTO. Instead of matching whatever fear or resistance they have and lowering your energy, you hold a powerful NEW space for them to step up. *When you value yourself first, others will follow.* It's a beautiful thing!

It truly is your mindset that creates your wealth. If you come from a background that has a foundation of scarcity and lack, you will be over-cautious when setting up your business. Your foundation of your business will be built on the same lack and scarcity that you learned as a child. Maybe you have the belief that someone doesn't have enough money for your services and so you keep yourself small.

A quick story about how I learned not to think about what others could or couldn't afford. While working in dentistry as a financial coordinator it was my job to sell the proposed treatment plan to the patients. One day the dentist proposed a ten thousand dollar treatment plan to an 83 year old woman. It was my job to seal the deal and get the cash. Truthfully, my money beliefs were built on lack and poverty, and so when I approached this patient I carried this belief with me and I assumed she would never go for it. Long story short, she agreed to treatment and the next day came in with ten thousand dollars in a brown paper back. She taught me to NEVER assume what anyone values or what they can afford. Making that decision about the woman was really a reflection of what was going on inside of me.

As a business owner it's not my job to worry how people will afford me. It's simply my job to show up ready to share the best me I can. I believe in what I offer and I know I am very skilled at what I do and so I charge what I'm worth. The feeling of worthiness has changed over the years for me and so has the way I do life and money!

#2 Master Your Money Moods

Uncover your inherited beliefs around money that are holding you back in business and in life.

In the last chapter I talked about how your money beliefs are holding you back, and in this chapter I want to go deeper into what those beliefs are and how to release them once and for all.

Look around - wealth is everywhere! Trust me, there is plenty of money and just because you're not seeing any of it doesn't mean it doesn't exist. Wealthy people live with a very wealthy frame of mind. I am not saying they didn't come from "a story"; I am saying they have all decided to develop the state of mind that instantly attracts more money.

Wealth cannot be pursued, it must be ATTRACTED.

Women Get Rich Because They Decide To... And They Take Inspired Action.

All the breaks you need in life wait within your imagination.

"Imagination is the workshop of your mind, capable of turning mind energy into accomplishment and wealth. "
Napoleon Hill

Anyone can somehow find money to buy whatever they **decide** to buy.

There is a misconception about exactly how much wealth there is floating around. If in fact you believe it's limited, you probably also believe that someone had to be at a loss for you to gain. This mind set will keep you broke. The truth is there is PLENTY of money and if you think there isn't, you aren't looking in the right places. Remember like attracts like.

Growing up I always believed we were poor. I always felt like a burden whenever I needed new shoes or school clothes. I now know my father was feeding his poverty mentality by holding on to his pennies. He was raised by depression era parents who put the fear of homelessness in him his whole life, and naturally this was a belief system he TRIED to give to me.

My father worked in a paper mill for 45 years and complained every single day. He was visibly miserable and I was determined NOT to inherit that same mentality. My father feared any RISK. **I look for RISK - because I know that's where the growth is.** My father was paralyzed by fear and that's what happens to a lot of people; they stay stuck believing one thing because they are terrified of believing something else.

I was always a square peg in a round hole. My entire life I questioned everything and conventionalism wasn't for me. I admit I stayed trapped in my father's belief system until I learned how to create a new mindset of my own. There was something to be said for the familiarity.

My new mindset was conceived out of pain - the pain of staying trapped in a way of life that made me feel uncomfortable. I knew that I wasn't supposed to be poor but I also knew acquiring riches was going to take a huge effort on my part and A LOT of courage. Thanks to some really great mentors and therapists I was able to figure out the emotional attachment I had to being broke. We are all searching to fulfill an underlying emotional need, sometimes unconsciously, sometimes consciously. My story with money involves LOTS of debt, $70K to be exact, and a lot of hitting bottom.

I didn't inherit the alcoholic gene from my father or the mental illness gene from my mother, but I did have an addiction - my addiction was compulsive spending. Whenever I felt ANYTHING, I would celebrate or soothe by buying something, and it didn't even have to be for me. I was very generous with my giving. The power of purchasing gave me the feeling of being somebody, of being worthy. My whole life I was cast aside and forgotten about, and when I bought stuff I felt powerful and relevant - I mattered.

I spent my 30's spending and soothing. It wasn't until I turned 40 and got divorced that I realize something had to give. I could not be a successful business owner and have these compulsive episodes - I had to figure out the root cause. While studying with one of my mentors, I discovered that I had the attachment to the money behavior because I kept recreating what was familiar to me - lack, scarcity, poverty, shame and guilt. Every time I'd spend money I'd experience a fleeting second of happiness, but the long term feelings were guilt and shame. Once I realized that, I looked even deeper, and I came to find out what I REALLY was looking for was recognition.

You see my whole life I was the one child who never fussed, who never gave my caregivers any problems. My brother was a sickly baby and required a lot of attention and care. He was fussed over and even spoiled, and to this day comes from a place of entitlement. Again, it's all he knows. The story I was told many times was how I was put to bed at 7pm and would sleep right through to till 7am and wake up covered in pee. Not a flattering story, but my caregivers tell that story from a place of love and I now recognize that and can get a chuckle from it.

Imagine my surprise at 47 years old realizing for the first time I longed to be recognized. THIS WAS POWERFUL! So powerful I decided to teach this to other women and to build my business on this one concept - it's never really about the money!

There Was Nowhere To Go But Up!

"Most great people have attained their greatest success just one step beyond their greatest failure." - Napoleon Hill, *Think and Grow Rich*

Before I realized that I was searching for recognition, things fell apart BIG TIME. I had been in business for a little over three and a half years, and while I was making some money, it was nowhere near what I wanted or needed to be making. I found myself becoming a recluse. I was holed up in my house constantly spinning in circles looking for the big break that I was certain would come in my inbox. I would buy (charge) everything that told me it was going to make me MONEY! I was physically harming myself with the dis-ease that was all over my life. I actually gained 30 pounds, became diabetic, got high blood pressure and sunk into a depression. I wasn't able to recognize how badly I was hurting myself. My life ached and I didn't know why.

Every day I'd wake up and go to my office and sit there with the intention of making that day be THE day. I had all the stuff one imagines an entrepreneur having - a website, an email marketing program, all the latest technology, a flip camera, a Facebook savvieness that earned me a loyal and consistent following, a formal education and so on. But something was wrong because every day without fail I would end up taking a nap. Yup - I'd "work" a bit and then I'd go lie down. Before long a short nap turned into an all afternoon nap. It was so bad that I would request my husband call me on his way home, so I could jump up and act as if I had been working. I was clearly depressed - but why?

The old saying, "It is always darkest before the dawn," rang true. All of the physical and mental ailments I experienced were compounded by the fact that my second husband was having an affair. That was it - I was officially broken open and all the dirty, festering anger and self-loathing, pissed off feelings toward myself and the world were flowing freely. I was fueled by revenge and the venom that oozed out of my being was most toxic to me!

I sunk to yet another low point in my life. The emotions and feelings surrounding that realization were unbearable. Here was this man that I had trusted more than anyone ever; someone who supported me unconditionally, both financially and emotionally, was gone from our marriage and I never even realized it. I was too lost in being lost. I am NOT in any way, shape, or form taking responsibility for his actions, but what I am taking responsibility for is my own behavior.

Suddenly, as if the curtains were drawn open, I saw light - I realized that NO ONE was ever going to fix this except me and I am not talking about the affair. I am talking about healing me. So, here I was again on another inward journey, an excavation. The tools to perform the excavation were the physical and mental stuff and the affair. If it weren't for the affair I may have never fully woken up.

So, what did it mean to wake up? It meant it was time to be a big girl and start dealing with my reality. The reality was I was a sickly, overweight recluse who drank too much, was $70K in debt, whose husband was cheating and I had a flop of a business. And, until you can get in a mirror and be brutally honest with yourself, NOTHING CHANGES. Damn it, I wasn't having this way of life anymore!

I'd like to say *Poof* in the blink of an eye I found success - BUT the saga continued for another year. I consider myself a fairly enlightened being, but boy, I sure was slow on "getting" it when it came to uncovering my success. I still had a way to go...more to learn.

The secret to having a prosperous life and business is that everything is interconnected. There is no separation between anything in your life. What I mean by that is one event is an effect or cause of another event. Yes, this is a business book, and I will reiterate, there is nothing separate - business and life are one.

I was always taught that you should compartmentalize your life. One thing had nothing to do with the other. So stubbing your toe after waking up late for work had nothing to do with the events that transpired throughout your day, or that fact that you cleverly hide from reality had nothing to do with a spouse having an affair. I say that facetiously because it is most certainly all connected.

Let me show you how using a business example. While I had all the "right" stuff to have a successful business I was broke and sick - why? If we go back to the idea that one thing effects everything here's how it goes.

On an energetic level I am living and breathing from a place of insecurity, desperation, frustration, blame and hate. I am barely tolerating those around me. I am finding fault with everyone in sight. Energetically I am throwing all that out to the universe and guess what? That is exactly what is coming back to me. It's showing up as illness, poverty, fear, disconnect and anger. You can say that's crazy and decide not to believe it, BUT that's the beauty of universal laws - they happen whether you believe in them or not. Let me just say, when I was "in" this energy I did not know it. It's like being in the eye of a hurricane.

I am a certified practitioner in the law of attraction so I knew this in an academic way, but was I applying it? Obviously NOT! Why? Because I really didn't believe it to my core. That can be the only answer there is, because once I decided to trust in this universal principle: feelings changed, thoughts changed, behavior changed, and life changed. This is the system I used to crawl back up and this is the very system I use to help clients create their own income. My motto in life and business is SIMPLICITY and trust me, it doesn't get any simpler than the law of attraction - that is, once you understand it fully.

Stress, worry, lack, scarcity, depravation.....all DIS-EASE to the body

The concept of mind over matter is not new. Forever we have heard stories of miraculous healing or how someone overcame some great physical limitation. With recent advances in science we can now chart the pathway of a thought down to the genes within each cell. This revelation is adding credibility to the concept of mind over matter.

What we are learning is that paying attention to our thoughts will allow us to change what were once thought to be pre-destined conditions. If we followed a thought on its journey, it would take us first through the brain and then into the body, and then all the way down to the genes themselves. We would see that thoughts do, in fact, influence health.

Recently I was reading an interview with Dr. Candice Pert, an internationally recognized pharmacologist, and the interviewer asked her what the interface or junction is where thoughts somehow affect us physically. Dr. Pert replied, "The emotions. The emotions are the currency of exchange between mind and body." If your emotions are the currency exchange between mind and body, and you were vibrating at a low level (negative, stressful thoughts), couldn't it possibly show up as dis-ease? The decaying or dis-easing of the body must first be a thought. Our thoughts are much more toxic now than ever with the stress of life in in our culture. What will you think yourself into?

What You Think About You Bring About: The Law of Attraction.

Let me break that down into simpler terms: if you have constant stress and negativity in your life, you will ALWAYS be filled with worry, angst and tension, and therefore will be vibrating at a lower frequency and drawing dis-ease (disease) to your body. However, if you make a conscious decision to focus on the positive, filled with love, tolerance and acceptance, you will ALWAYS find all of that woven throughout your life and health.

**Another way to think about The Law of Attraction is that what you consistently think about and what moves you to emotion is what you will bring forward in your life.**

The Law doesn't differentiate between good emotions and bad ones. If you want something _really badly_ (simple terms) and _feel really good_ about it, you will most likely get it. On the other hand, if you _do not_ want something, and _feel bad about the prospect of having it, you will probably get it, too!_

The above example seems very simplistic and almost "hokey," but there is scientific proof behind the words. Keeping it simple, here is my attempt at an explanation. Everything around us vibrates; every piece of existence is a form of electro-magnetic energy. This is a scientific fact. Even we are made up of energy. Ever have an MRI or EKG? That's your energy!

Everything in the Universe is made up of atoms and every atom in the Universe is made of sub-atomic particles. Every sub-atomic particle is made up of energy or light which can be subdivided into particles or waves. These particles or waves are flashing constantly in and out of existence millions of times a second. Think about what it looks like when you flick the lights off and on, or picture a strobe light. Essentially that means the entire Universe is like a giant hologram flashing continuously. This all happens so quickly we can't see it.

Every thought interacts with the energy of the universe. Negative thought looks for other negative thought energies to connect with. They connect by the frequency at which they vibrate. *Negative energy is lower vibration because it is denser and heavier.* An environment of negative thought energy is created and forms a thought wave. These powerful negative thought waves manifest themselves in our lives in the form of poverty, crime, and war, etc. Negative energy detracts from the *life-giving nature* of the universe. You will recognize the labels we give negative thoughts: bad luck, misfortune, disaster, evil, curses, etc. The source of all of this resides within us! Remember, it's *what you think about.*

On the "up" side, positive thought energy also seeks out other positive energies. If you are a source of positive thought energy, positive and beneficial energy will return to you in many wonderful ways. Everything that happens in your life has a direct connection with the type of energy that you are charging the universe with. *Positive energy is higher vibration because it is finer and lighter.* Think about what it feels like to be happy, or in love. Light and airy - there's buoyancy about you. You alone are responsible for the type of energy created by your life!

In order to create a new way you must first transform.

Steps to help you transform

Insight: A tree begins with a seed. Insight is your seed.

Timing: Timing is REALLY everything. A seed knows when to bloom, birds know when to migrate. Know yourself, know your timing. Get quiet. Develop excellent timing through silence.

Patience: Only humans are impatient. Know yourself. Don't rush divine order. Know when to bloom.

Surrender: Let go of the NEED to control. Let go of your story. Spiritually surrender to a Higher Power.

Grounding: If a tree has deep roots, it is stronger. The same is true for you. Immerse yourself in something bigger than you: Books, CD's, workshops, etc.

Balance: Even when the tree is firmly rooted it still needs balance, the correct amount of water, light and food.

Growth: When given the correct amount of what it needs, the tree automatically grows. When you feed yourself by all of the above you will evolve naturally.

Transformation: The seeds of your insight will take root and you will know the glow of traveling the highest path.

"We are confronted with insurmountable opportunities."
Walt Kelly

Before you can release anything you must first become intimate with it. Recognize it, and in order to recognize it you must ask questions. Here are a few questions to help you begin the process of awareness:

- ✓ What am I willing to let go of?
- ✓ Is there something that has been sabotaging my efforts to live from my Soul?

✓ What experiences do I long for today? This yearning becomes your intention for the week. Practice listening to your inner voice. Sit quietly and let spirit guide you.

✓ How might fear stop me from achieving my intention? Fear blocks you from trusting your intuition. List all your fears surrounding your intention.

✓ What would help my body feel loved this week? Get quiet and ask your body what it needs from you.

✓ What kind of self-talk have I been using lately? Am I kind and loving to myself or am I critical and demanding? Explore your self-talk with words.

✓ Today I am grateful for..........

The Key to Financial Freedom

Now that you have an understanding of the law of attraction, let's look at the emotional side of having the money you desire and deserve.

All of us inherit a money story/belief. I mentioned that mine was one of scarce and lack. Here is an excellent way to see your money story. Take out your wallet and examine it. Describe the condition it's in - not just the physical description, color, size but the way it presents. Is it messy, super organized, too full, nothing in it? Now take a look at how your life/business is a reflection of that wallet. Surprising, yes?

How you do money is how you do life - how you do EVERYTHING. Your money beliefs are woven throughout every aspect of your existence: relationships, business, hopes, dreams, desires. If you are haphazard and disrespectful with money, chances are you live life and do business that way too. If you are overly calculating and overly conservative with money that is probably how you live life and do business. You cannot escape your money beliefs - until you become aware of them.

I had no respect for money and always just knew more would show up. I spent way more than I had because I had such a lack of respect. Also a part of me was rebelling against my family legacy of lack. My wallet was frequently over flowing with receipts, and money (when I had it) was haphazardly balled up inside. I was barely able to close it most days and often struggled to find anything in it. As I stood back and observed my life, it too was exactly like my wallet. Haphazard, out of balance, no self-respect, and I struggled to fit it all in, and as a result was disorganized! What a gift when my eyes were opened to this concept.

Embracing the paradigm of "How you do money is how you do everything" really changed my life. I began to look deeper into my emotional need that was tied to money.

The real reason people don't have any more or have less than they would like is because they are unconsciously blocking themselves from having it, and that block comes from an unmet need. I am NOT a psychologist but I have personally been taught this concept by my mentor, Kendall Summerhawk, who is a brilliant soul and teacher. When she walked me through this process on a live call I had no idea my life (and income level) would forever change. Our unconscious, unmet need is often found in one of the following five words - Love, Security, Recognition, Validation, Status...This is how I found out that my behavior of inflicting shame and guilt on myself came out of my unmet need for recognition. Because of this process (which I now teach) I was able to reframe my money belief and release what was holding me back. I embraced the fact that I yearned for recognition and I was able to give myself permission to feel worthy of standing up and being recognized. The proof is in the revelations - the "a-ha's." This realization coupled with strong practical business systems I am a successful entrepreneur - FINALLY!

To begin this process, I encourage you to take a look at your family money legacy. Become intimate with your story. Decide if it works for you or not. Below are a few questions to help you begin the process:

- ✓ What money story were you taught as a child?
- ✓ Can you identify ways it's shown up in your life?
- ✓ Who gave you that money story?
- ✓ Can you see they had good intentions for giving it to you?
- ✓ What can you be grateful to that person for?

This is the freedom and permission you need to move past the lack in your business. The rest is just systems - "how-to's" - so let's get to it!

Section Two

The next section of this book contains the practical "how to's" that allowed me to create my business.

#3: Define the Sweet Spot in Your Business by Identifying Your Unique Tribe

Discover how to instantly and effortlessly attract your ideal client.

The Key to your success is KNOWING EXACTLY who your client is!

I am going to share with you how to create an authentic niche that's going to help you sell more of everything and position you as the **go-to expert** in your field. There is a very specific formula for finding exactly who you are meant to serve.

BEFORE YOU GO ANY FURTHER, YOU MUST UNDERLINE THIS - JOT IT DOWN - MEMORIZE IT: BEFORE YOU DEFINE THE WHAT YOU DO, YOU MUST KNOW THE WHO!

What exactly does that mean? More often than not, most business owners start out with what they have or create what they want to give to the world. I am suggesting you reverse that thought process. Before you create your service/product I urge you to identify exactly WHO your prospective clients are.

Maybe you already have a niche, or you may be wondering what your niche is. You may want to fine tune your niche or possibly you are asking, "What is a niche?" **A niche** is the service you specialize in offering to your target market.

Your niche is a combination of three things.

- The people you serve.

- The problem you help them solve.

- Your special system; your "signature series."

Why is it so important to clearly define your niche?

Imagine yourself going into a convention for hair stylists and you start trying to sell medical equipment. Doesn't make any sense, does it? This is EXACTLY what happens when you aren't sure exactly who you are sharing your brand with.

Once you know exactly who you are "talking" to you will know exactly what to say, because you will have researched and become familiar with your niche.

Areas to explore surrounding your desired niche:

- What are **their struggles?**

- What are **their fears?**

- What **motivates them?**

- Can they **afford** you?

- What results are **they looking for?**

- What is it **costing them** (emotionally) to stay stuck?

When people understand how you **can help them** and you're offering something that they want and are willing to pay for, that's what leads to more sales, higher fees and being THE GO-TO-EXPERT. **PEOPLE BUY RESULTS TO PROBLEMS THEY ARE EXPERIENCING.**

One of the benefits of niching your business is that you will instantly be on the path to expert status.

I am a firm believe that MINDSET rules everything we do. I want to show how to simply shift into expert mindset.

There are two ways to see your future- as a specialist or a generalist. Where do you think you can transform the most lives?

➤ A generalist is all things to all people.

➤ A specialist is focused on one very specific area.

➤ Generalist have a one size fits all mentality.

➤ Specialists tailor everything they do/offer to meet the needs of a specified group.

➤ THINK in terms of retail:

   Walmart clothing vs. Ann Taylor

➤ THINK in terms of teeth: You have a toothache and you need a root canal - you go to an endodontist who specializes in root canals.

➤ THINK in terms of cars: You drive a Toyota - you take your car to a mechanic who specializes in Toyotas. Just makes sense.

Being a generalist does not allow you to do business with intensity … you are too scattered.

Being a specialist is a combination of 3 things:

✓ Confidence

✓ High quality work skills

✓ Passion about what you do and who you serve

Here are few questions to help you identify if you are a specialist:

1. Is most of your business focused on one specific topic?

2. Do your peers call you when they have a question on this one topic?

3. Have you written a book on a specific topic?

4. Do reporters call on you for quotes on a specific topic?

5. Do you speak at industry events on a specific topic?

6. Do you write regularly on a specific topic?

Your Niche Is Your Tribe - Build It and They Will Come!

I realize the very idea of getting so specific terrifies you - I WAS YOU. I promise you, once you know who you are talking to specifically you will thrive.

Since the beginning of time, humans have belonged to tribes. Being a business owner is all about finding your tribe and effectively and confidently leading them.

Tribes are based on FAITH - a belief in an idea and in a community.

Knowing your niche will define and call up your tribe.

Top 4 Reasons to NICHE your business:

1. Fewer competitors

2. Ability to be more efficient

3. More profitable

4. Increase visibility

Let me give you an example - financial advisors. Lots of them out there. Distinguishing yourself from the crowd is what will create sales.

Let me show you how to get really narrow with this niche - the financial advisor who concentrates on retirement for people who care for a disabled loved one. Instantly the competition melts away.

The benefits of a Financial Advisor who specializes in estate planning - she only needs to be well versed in estate planning, NOT college funds or how to finance a business. JUST estate planning - she is the expert.

See how much better she can serve her client with a concentration on one specialty?

Remember, if you are like everyone else you will market like everyone else! Embrace your uniqueness and NICHE.

I want to walk you through an exercise now to help you hone in on what you are really great at, and what you are comfortable enough in to call yourself an expert.

Pull out your resume and use it as a guide.

Typically we don't list every job we have - but for this exercise I want you to list everything, even volunteer work.

Take a piece of paper and create 5 columns.

1. List every job you ever had.

2. Write out job duties for each job - a complete list of what you did while in that role. DO NOT restrict

yourself. Forget your title and focus on what you actually did.

3. Next review your skill set for every duty you performed. List the top 3 skills you acquired while doing that job.

4. Next column write out hobbies, recreational activities - list all the skills you needed.

5. Last column paint a picture of all the skill sets you have acquired over time.

6. Take the single top skill that appears over and over and use it to help solidify your expert status - your niche. This is critical to building your brand and your niche.

Another example of niches:

Ben & Jerry's VS Häagen Dazs- these 2 have very separate markets.

Feel the difference - Ben & Jerry's appeals to the free spirit /hippy, while Häagen Dazs is more sophisticated in its marketing.

By knowing who they are trying to reach they can then talk their language. (This doesn't mean hippies won't buy Häagen Dazs!)

Here is the ultimate example of having a niche and tribe to follow.

There is a restaurant in Brooklyn that only opens 20 times a year and always on a Saturday night. The ONLY way you can go is by going online, securing an appointment/reservation and PAYING for it right then and there.

These business owners can now fill the house with diners. Their following knows this, and instead of cooking dishes for anonymous people they are throwing a party and people pay to come! More than a restaurant, this has become a tribal meeting place ...sharing, laughing and enjoying great food! They have a thriving business totally by word of mouth - the tribe breeds itself organically.

The owners built their tribe via their popular food blog and website and then they built their restaurant. Constant interaction with their tribe. RELATIONSHIPS!

I know firsthand how scary it is when you first sit down to look at your niche and begin tweaking it. Most of us go into our story- our fears surface and we can become paralyzed with fear, and that often keeps us stuck. The fear is in part due to the fact that you know you're going to be leaving behind old beliefs and ideas that are comfortable and familiar but no longer serve you. If YOU are going to step up and BE what your clients need, you are going to have to grow past what you know!

If you're brand-new to business, you want to figure out what your place and path are. Who are you meant to serve, and in what way are you meant to serve? This is the FOUNDATION of building ANY business; miss this step and it's like shooting at a moving target.

Tip: If you are a seasoned business owner I strongly suggest you re-evaluate your niche and perhaps look for sub-niche categories to serve more people. As a business owner you always want to be thinking who and what is next.

Stepping into something that's new is uncomfortable. Remember, it's only uncomfortable because it is new. That's all.

Tip: Jump into this with your whole heart and soul. The sooner you jump into a clearly defined niche, the sooner you are going to make money.

Everything we do in business and in life begins without mindset. I'm going to ask you to be open to making some important mindset shifts.

Remember- The more you grow, the more your business will grow. Growing yourself and business means being willing to let go of the old and step into a new version of yourself.

- Shift #1: Be willing to see and feel things in a new way. Be open to feeling uncomfortable and maybe even a little scared. It's OK, we've ALL been there.

- Shift #2: BE DECISIVE & BE BOLD. A lot of women fail to find their niche because they do not want to exclude anybody. They think they can be all things to all people. **THEY ARE AFRAID THEY'LL MISS AN OPPORTUNITY TO MAKE MONEY, when in reality they are so scattered they are missing A LOT of money not being specific and committed.**

Nice To Meet You, "What Do You Do?"

How many times have you met someone new and they asked you "what do you do" and you tell them YOUR TITLE? Most entrepreneurs think that they are in the business of being

THEIR TITLE - whatever the thing is that they do. When people ask them, "What do you do?, "they answer, "I'm a coach," "a shop owner", or "trainer," or "speaker." This isn't what you do, and it's not the business you're in. What do I mean by this?

Here is an example:

There was a man whose business was installing home security systems. He was doing very well until people realized they could go to a home improvement store and install their own systems. Obviously, this hurt his bottom line, but being the consummate entrepreneur he sat with the facts of situation and came up with **WHAT HE WAS REALLY IN THE BUSINESS OF.** It wasn't home security - that was simple a byproduct of what he REALLY DID. Simply put, he was **in the business of putting holes in the wall and running wire.** Take away the fluff and you can see how he stripped it all down to the bareness of what he was **REALLY** doing: punching holes and running wires. When he got that clarity he began to think of other ways he could take his skill set and make it a business.

He quickly began looking for opportunities to put holes in the wall. He eventually came up with installing home theaters. Brilliant, yes. **Holes in the wall and running wires**! Not only did he install but he soon built his empire on other areas of that particular business. He sold equipment and furniture for the rooms, helped design rooms and so on. This entrepreneur did not limit himself to the title of Home Security Installer, and because he stepped back and saw the BIG picture he found more ways to serve which meant more income.

TIP: You limit yourself and the people you can potentially serve when you are being just your title. Think out of the box about what you really do.

How to Discover the Business You Are REALLY In

Here is where a mind shift comes into play. Instead of saying "I am _____ (insert title)," instead complete this sentence: "I am in the business of _____."

Feel how expansive that feels. It literally opens up so many more opportunities.

An example:

I am an organizer vs. **I am in the business of organizing business and creating systems**. Can you see how clear and defined the "in the business" statement is vs. the "title statement"?

Take some time to process this and fill in the blank for yourself.

I am in the business of

_____.

NOTE: This is not your elevator speech or what you put on a business card. This IS PURELY for you to get clear on who you serve and what you actually do. This is your inner work just for you. This is your brainstorming session. Framing it like this will allow you to see your business through new eyes and help you get a shift in perspective.

Who Can You Potentially Serve?
This is a short and sweet BUT powerful exercise.

Create a short list of your highest potential people to work with. Keep this list general for now. Once you come up with some general categories, break those down even further.

Example:

- ✓ Entrepreneurs
- ✓ Coaches
- ✓ Restaurant owners

Next, break it down even further:

- ✓ Entrepreneurs who are women who are brand new to business
- ✓ Coaches that specialize in relationships; marital relationships
- ✓ Restaurant owners who specialize in outdoor dining on the west coast

Can you see how much clarity there is? And as you begin to drill down you will get even clearer on who you serve.

By now, what you want to have is the "I am in the business of _____" statement and five, six or seven general categories.

Tips on finding your niche

- Identify a SPECIFIC TYPE of person (s) you want to serve. Don't censor yourself. Come up with several choices to choose from.

- Step out of the box - go **OUTSIDE of your normal area**. For example, if you are a make-up rep, brainstorm how your service can help women in corporations, small business owners, executives. You'll be surprised at how this will help you gain a new perspective into new groups of people that you may not have previously thought of, and will help you see how your services can benefit people who have the money to pay you handsomely.

Take your time and play around. Brainstorm! Figure out what will resonate the most with you. You may initially come up with 50 different options before it becomes crystal clear to you.

Make sure to NOT over think this process. Let it flow organically and be mindful of the fact that you can ALWAYS change your mind!

TIP: When selecting your niche you want to do some research on their ability to afford your services. This is where your research comes in.

How to determine if your potential niche can support you:

- Typically there should be at least 10,000 people or more in order to have a viable niche.

- Make sure you are flowing in the same direction with your prospective clients; "you can't teach an old dog new tricks." It will be much easier for you to find success if you are with the flow of your niche's culture.

- How important is it to people within your prospective niche to solve this problem? On a scale of 1-10, where do they come in?

- What is your prospective client investing in: continuing education, model airplanes? Is it relevant to your services?

- Lastly, and MOST IMPORTANT - do you LOVE your prospective clients? You will be working very closely with them and it's important for your values to match your prospects.

#4: Develop Your Authentic and Compelling Brand Statement

Discover how to become a leader of influence in your industry using a unique phrase that speaks to your audience.

Branding links your passions, key personal attributes, and strengths with your value proposition, in a crystal clear message that differentiates your unique promise of value from your peers and resonates with your target audience. It is typically one or two sentences in length.

Your branding statement communicates the essence of who you are in your industry. Your brand reflects your professional reputation — it's defines exactly what you are the expert in, what you're known for (or would like to be known for). A strong branding statement is a way to stand out from the masses.

Breaking it down, branding statements explain:

- Your specialty — who you are
- Your service — what you do
- Your audience — who you do it for
- Your best characteristic — what you're known for

Put all the pieces together, and you end up with something a little like this:

"I'm an Intuitive Business Consultant who helps fast paced, creative, emerging entrepreneurial women create a strong personal

economy for themselves using my intuition and business background." Veronica Drake

You can use your branding statements in the following ways:

- Cover letters, online profiles, and social media
- Printed on the back of business cards
- As part of your elevator speech
- "Tell me about yourself" situations
- Networking

An extra benefit of writing a branding statement is the clarity it helps to create. It is a way of getting crystal clear on who you are and what you do!

The Simple Secret That Will Position You as the Go-To Expert

We live in a very tuned-in, highly sophisticated world where the consumer is leery to spend if they can't instantly see / feel value. Your #1 job as a business owner is to create the value that will transform your prospects' lives.

The biggest mistake you can make is promoting without a crystal clear message, and you cannot be crystal clear if you are a one-size-fits-all messenger.

Knowing your niche will empower you to create great marketing messages. The ideal message differentiates you from all your competitors. This is your Unique Selling Proposition (USP) - without this you are SIMPLY ONE MORE CHOICE in an already crowded marketplace. Think of your

USP as your position against your competition and against all other choices.

Think Walmart - they are the low price leader.

The way to identify your USP is to highlight one of your benefits.

Your USP can express the theme of your business.

USP can feature pricing, product positioning, color, scent, size, location, hours of operation.

Think benefits - transformational value.

To learn more about creating a USP take a look around you - the places you do business with.

Become USP sensitive.

- ✓ See if you can identify the USP of a particular place of business

- ✓ If not, create one for them.

- ✓ If you can identify, it can you make it better?

- ✓ Is there any idea YOU CAN BORROW for your business?

Take a few minutes and see if you can identify these USPs:

Domino's – "Delivered in 30 minutes or less or it's free."

FedEx - "When it absolutely, positively has to be there overnight."

M&Ms – "The milk chocolate melts in your mouth, not in your hand."

Instantly recognizable!

#5: Mastering the Art of Writing Effective Copy

Discover exactly how to position yourself as the go-to expert in your industry using the written word.

What Exactly Is Copy?

"Sell a good night's sleep - not the mattress." I love this quote. It articulates the fact that what we are offering is **never about us** - it is about the **results and the benefits** your services/products offer **to your prospects**. Great copy doesn't just happen, it is conceived.

Basic definition of copy: Salesmanship in print. Imagine hiring and PAYING a door-to-door salesperson and they never make any sales. You'd either retrain them or fire them! BUT that is essentially what you are doing if your website isn't selling for you.

Just to clarify: copy writing and copyrighting are two very different acts.

Copywriting: The act of writing copy (text) for the purpose of advertising or marketing a product, business, person, opinion or idea.

Copyrighting: The exclusive legal right, given to an originator or an assignee to print, publish, perform, film, or record literary, artistic.

The Power of Copy

From now on you must think of yourself as being an online marketer **of your programs and services**. I know… We all dislike the marketing aspect, BUT it is a very crucial component to our survival. The sooner you embrace the mindset of a marketer the sooner you will attract more clients and gain expert status!

Think Of Your Website as a Sales Letter

One of two things happens when someone visits your site:

1. You are selling the visitor your product.

2. They are selling themselves the idea that they don't need to buy your product.

You web page is a long scrolling body of copy that tells a story. When all the relevant pieces are in harmony and when done properly, it will produce a beautiful melody to your clients' ears!

You do not have to be a proficient writer - all you need to be is interested in selling your services and adding transformational value to your clients' lives.

You will need to show up willing and ready to engage your creativity. **It is imperative that you KNOW your niche. Knowing who you are talking to is what makes compelling copy that sells.** If you are struggling with your niche, no worries - you can check out my Client Attraction VIP Day. It's filled with step by step processes to gain clarity on your niche.

Turning Words Into Dollars

If the copy on your site is not making enough sales (minimally 1% conversion rate - that is, 1 out of every 100 visitors should buy something) you either need to tweak your copy or get new copy!

There are four key tasks your copy must accomplish:

1. **Your copy MUST get your reader's Attention.** Your headline must grab your reader's eyes and draw them into your site! It must be compelling, intriguing and RELEVANT to their issue!

2. **Your copy MUST keep your reader's Interest.** The body of your copy must tell a story that is captivating to them! The body speaks their language.

3. **Your copy MUST arouse your reader's Desire and curiosity.** Presenting a great logical case for your service or product is NOT enough. Your copy must stir up a desire and feeling that produces an emotional connection.

4. **Your copy MUST entice your reader to take Action.** The goal of your copy is to get visitors to take action when they visit your site. This action can be to BUY or to OPT IN.

Attention + Interest + Desire = Action

"There is more similarity in the marketing challenge of selling a precious painting by Degas and a frosted mug of root beer than you ever thought possible." – A. Alfred Taubman

This is the time-tested proven recipe for successful copy. I can hear you now - "I already know this" ... "my services are different"..."I want something cutting edge - really out of the box." Whatever your excuse is, it's not going to work with me!

THIS IS THE FORMULA TO CREATING GREAT COPY THAT SELLS.

Must Haves for Great Copy

1. The Pre-Header

The pre-head is at the top of the sales letter/website (mindset: sales letter & website copy are synonymous) and it's usually a sentence fragment.

Short, simple and to the point. The pre-header is there to capture attention.

It might look something like this: **"Attention Women Entrepreneurs!"** If you're a woman entrepreneur, that will grab your attention.

If you have a service that's designed to help people with their new puppies, the pre-header could simply be: **"Calling All Puppy Owners!"** To make it even more specific (I'm a stickler for niching) you could focus on all owners of Boxer puppies - **"Attention All Owners of Boxer Puppies"**. See how clear and concise that feels? The clearer you are, the easier writing copy will be and the easier you will increase sales.

"It's not thinking about the reader, but being able to look at it as if you were the reader. See things through the reader's eyes ... and write what the reader wants to hear."– David Deutsch

2. The Headline

The headline's job is to keep the reader reading. Get them to read the next sentence and the next. Grab their attention by talking their language!

Statistically speaking, **you have two to five seconds to grab the attention of people who are coming to your site for the first time.** That's how long it's going to take them to decide whether they're going to keep on reading or not. In many cases, they're going to click the button and be gone. Google analytics will help you see your own stats.

Think of your headline as your first introduction. Imagine yourself at a dinner party and you are meeting someone for the first time. You want the headline to evoke feelings. Choosing the right words comes easily when you KNOW your prospect. The way to know them is to research them. I'll share tips on how to do that later in this book.

An effective headline has four purposes and they must all work together to create a successful headline:

- Starts a relationship with your prospects
- Delivers a complete message
- Compels your reader to read more
- Grabs your prospect's attention

Michael Masterson of American Writers and Artists (AWAI) specified that great headlines should include the four U's:

- Uniqueness – don't offer the same old thing everyone else is offering.

- Urgent – if you can tie your headline to some form of urgency, that's great.

- Useful – provide information to indicate to your reader that if they keep on reading, they will learn something they can use.

- Ultra Specific – use numbers when you can, and don't round them up or down.

I am a huge fan of long headlines! The more enticing, the better conversions.

Example:

"You're About To Learn Secrets That Most People Will Never Know About How To Really Attract Wealth into Their Lives!"

Your Turn

Create your own headline, substituting info from your niche where I have indicated with parentheses. "**You're About to Learn Secrets That Most** (enter a descriptive term for your market, such as 'entrepreneurs, single mothers, aspiring fishermen, beginning quilters') **Will Never Know About How To Really** (list a benefit that your market really wants to have)!"

Two very important tips to remember:

1) **Do your research! This will solidify your copy.** Use the internet, local newspapers, "expert" magazines; interview the experts. The more you research, the stronger your copy will be. Keep a file of your resources for future writing.

2) **Know Your Niche!** Create a prospective buyer profile. Who are they… Where do they hang out…What are their problems… Then, dig deeper and start to think about your prospects' beliefs, feelings, and desires. Find out what keeps your prospect awake at night! Your service/product IS the solution they are searching for! This is GOLD!

3. The Subheader

The sub header is a block of type that is usually bolded and set apart from the rest of the text. It comes between the headline and the beginning of the letter.

The subheader is to **support and reinforce the impact of the idea proposed in the headline** and to also arouse more curiosity.

Ways to think about subheaders:

- **Explanatory subheaders:** Subheaders can be slightly longer than headings (you are expanding on the header). They should provide a good frame for the context.

- **Directional subheaders:** Readers should be able to skim subheaders to get an idea of the content.

Example:

- ✓ Go From Broke to Billionaire Instantly
- ✓ Burn Disease Out Of Your Body
- ✓ Critical Info Most Business Coaches Don't Tell You About
- ✓ Fearless Conversation That Will Change Your Relationship

These are smaller headlines that separate the major sections of your sales letter. They connect the "dots" for the reader. They lead your reader through the body of your copy, and succinctly and briefly outline the point of the message.

Facts about readers:

- They never really read at first.
- They never believe anything the first time through.
- They never do anything the first time through your copy.

What they will do is look at your headline and IF that grabs them they will skim the rest; subheaders give them a general idea of what you are saying. While they are skimming, they are looking for words that scream out to them...that interest them...that are relevant to solving their problem. IF you capture them in this phase next they will read you.

Today's consumer is very savvy. They never believe anything at first read. Your job is to tell a story up front that resonates with them. **Build a genuine relationship**.

Observe your own experience when you're online and searching for something. Take time and list out exactly what you do.

4. The Body

This is the bulk of your text. This comprises most of your sales letter. The remaining components are all within the body: **The Lead, Rapport, Credibility, Bullets, Testimonials.**

TIP: Here's how to do the research to write your copy for your body. Do a Google search on your prospects (Example: search "Boxers" as well as "Boxer owner", "Boxer lover", "Boxer training", etc.). Next put together what your market is looking for and start searching for keywords that they might search for. In other words, pretend you're a Boxer owner wanting to find out what's available for your puppy.

Another way to research is to find your prospects in blogs. For example if you teach stay at home moms how to knit, you would find forums/blogs/chat rooms where they "hang out". These are great places where people are discussing your topic. Lots of learning! Just observe...read the threads in the discussion forums and see what people are talking about and what topics keep coming up over and over again.

Here is a great story from a copy writer/marketer attending one of his first seminars. He was taking notes, but not very many notes. Someone with him asked him, "Why aren't you getting much out of this?" He said, "It's great! I'm getting a lot out of this!" His friend said, "But you're not taking very many notes." He said, "Oh, I'm just **writing down the questions that people are asking**. That's how I'm going to know what services and products to create."

5. **The Lead**

This is the **beginning of the body of the sales letter/web copy.** This is the part that comes after "Dear ____". It can be one paragraph, two or several. Sometimes it consists of a simple "if, then" or "what if" statement; sometimes it consists of a story that is intended to persuade you to a certain way of thinking.

The lead defines who the letter is intended for and what they will get out of reading it. Remember WIIFM (What's In It For Me). Here is an example of a classic lead: "If you've struggled to consistently attract the ideal client and increase your bottom line, you are probably making the #1 mistake new entrepreneurs make over and over again. Learn how to break the cycle NOW and stop struggling:"

That's a lead. Does it do what we just talked about? Does it set the criteria of who the letter is for? Does it tell you what you stand to gain by reading the letter?

6. Rapport

This is relationship building. It's extremely important your reader feels connected to you. This is how you build the know, like and trust factor.

Rapport demonstrates that you know the reader's pain; that you understand their problems and that you have some common experiences that you can share that proves you understand their pain.

ALWAYS be authentic with your relationships! You should truly LOVE your niche. Love spending time with them and getting to know them.

7. Bullet Points

Very simply put, a bullet is a brief statement that identifies a single benefit offered by your product or service. Bullet points are extremely easy to read. There's lots of white space around them, they're short, they're punchy and if you format them correctly, someone can gather a lot of information by scanning over bullets very quickly.

Copy that converts at a high rate (makes a lot of sales) usually has a lot of bullets. Bullets are very powerful sales tools.

Why Bullet Points?

The purpose of a bullet point is to create that curious reaction that makes you think, "I've got to know what that is!"

Bullet points:

- Allow the reader to quickly scan and still get the information

- Highlight the main points you want your reader to remember

- Provide bite-sized pieces of information that engage your reader

- Easily summarize the main benefits of your product or service

- Highlight key points and important information that catch the readers' eye

- Break up the writing on a page, making it more inviting to read

- Sneak facts into your copy in a compelling way

- Are difficult for most readers to skip over or ignore

Pay particular attention to bullet points that catch YOUR eye, as well as those from successful marketers in your niche or market.

To create bullet points for your own products and services, here are some simple steps:

- List the benefits of your product or service. Tell the readers what positive changes they can expect when they do whatever it is you want them to do.
- Note any specific details or facts that you can mention to provide specificity (offering specific details lends credibility to your bullet point).
- Think of some questions your potential customers might have. Then ask them in an interesting manner.

8. Testimonials

This is third party verification that your solution does what it claims to do. These third parties are credible people who know - in other words, people who have used your product or service, liked it and are willing to endorse it.

Make sure to include the full name, not just initials, and a photo if possible. A full name gives stronger credibility. Also listing their website or contact info is applicable.

If you're just starting out, you may not have any testimonials yet. In this case, you could use quotes from famous people, as long as it's clear you're not implying that the famous person is personally endorsing your product.

Example, if you have a product about doing better advertising, you could include this quote from Mark Twain inside a testimonial box: *"Many a small thing has been made large by the right kind of advertising."*

#6: Engage Your Inner Goddess to Tell Your Compelling Story

Learn how to create a heartfelt bio and branding statement that will make you memorable.

Your bio is your story. I am not one for hard core stuffy bios. I am more the fluffy really reveal yourself kick your shoes off and get to know me bios. I feel writing this way is more genuine and people can begin to see inside of you.

Writing Your Bio

When creating your business, one of the most important tasks is creating your bio page. Your bio page is quite possibly the most important page of your site. It's where you define yourself to an audience, and where the process of know, like and trust begins. I am going to take you step by step through the sometimes daunting process of writing a heartfelt bio that will have your prospects wanting to spend time and money with you!

Before You Put Words to Paper

- Think about your audience. Your bio is for them; it is a tool for your audience to determine if your expertise and interests align with their needs. If your reader resonates with your bio they will begin the process of becoming acquainted with you.

- Give conscious thought to the impression you want people to have when reading your bio and the action you want them to take. How can you create a page that will feed these goals?

Writing About Yourself

- The biggest job your bio has is to communicate what makes you distinctive. Of all the people out there in your field, why should someone keep reading your bio? Do you have a distinct talent? Do you have a prestigious award or ranking to your credit? Are you an innovator in a particular respect? Consider leading with what makes you special.

- Always remain credible. If you make a claim, back it up with the facts (via hyperlink). For example, if you say your company is "award-winning," clarify which award or hyperlink the term "award-winning" to the award announcement.

- A bio is not a resume! You may certainly summarize your professional history, but you also want to give a sense of your professional philosophy, your areas of interest and expertise and your personality. Keep it real - down to earth - show heart.

- One of the best ways to show your heart is to tell a story - your story. Consider all the things that make a story compelling. Engage your audience in the tale of how you became who you are, or how you do what you do.

- Having someone take the time to read your bio page is just the beginning of a relationship. This is where story and personality are critical, as those are some of the building blocks of relationships. **SHOW YOUR PERSONALITY!**

- Share some details about your non-work life. If you are a marathon runner, or you do volunteer work, share it at the end. It adds another dimension to your personality and gives your audience a fuller sense of who you are.

What's Your Style?

- Always write in the first person. There is a big debate when it comes to bios whether to write in first or third person. I am definitely of the mindset that your bio is YOUR story and you should be telling it! First person!

- Share your accomplishments with humility. Don't "over toot" your own horn - this can be a real turn off.

- Your writing style should reflect your personality, but your first consideration should be your audience. Typically your clients are you 3-5 steps ago, so when you share yourself, those who are drawn to you will resonate with your tone.

- Use your words meaningfully. Avoid jargon that may confuse or alienate people who are unfamiliar with its meaning. Keep it simple!

#7: Identify and Access Your Most Profitable Marketplace

Discover how to position yourself as the go-to expert in your industry.

People Will First and Foremost Buy Your WHY

What is your WHY?

Every single business knows WHAT they do. Some know HOW they do it. Few businesses know WHY they do what they do.

Think of your WHY in these terms: "What's your purpose, your cause, your belief; why do you get out of bed in the morning; why should anyone care?"

Most people start with the WHAT, go to the HOW, and end with the WHY. That was the old way of doing business. As we all step into our more enlightened, feminine energy we are learning to put our WHY out there. Lead with your WHY!

What You Do vs. Why You Do It

Examples of the difference

My "What I Do"

I have 20 years' experience in building businesses and creating systems for business owners. I have a strong ability in product creation and development. I support businesses using my seasoned managerial background and experience in PR and Marketing.

My "Why I do it"

I am passionate about helping women business owners create their own economy so that they can consistently care for their families. I thrive on finding out- of-the-box ways and systems to support women to build stronger businesses.

I love helping women find solutions that make their lives easier in general. I encourage women to believe in themselves by offering up a safe space for them to experiment and grow personally and professionally.

Defining Your WHY Example:

Apple Computer is a great example of a company that operates from the inside out. Follow along and feel the difference.

What if Apple said, *"We make great computers. They are simple to use and easy to buy. So go get yourself an Apple Computer."*

UNINSPIRING! This is how MOST businesses market their products. They forget to make you FEEL something.

What if they said, *"In everything we do, we believe in challenging the status quo. By challenging the status quo we make our products very user friendly, make them simple to buy and ensure that each one is beautifully designed. Our computers are great, wanna buy one?"*

Feel the difference between the two? The second is Apple's style. They make you feel something and that is why most people buy — because they feel.

Take Your Time

Defining your WHY is a big step and should not be rushed. You should take time to be quiet and still and search deeply inside yourself for WHY you have decided to do the work you do. Infuse heart into your marketing by defining your WHY.

Essential Marketing Steps

What does it takes to attract customers?

As a business, you need to have a strong grasp on what it takes to attract customers. I will help you discover the essential marketing steps that will continue to be valuable to you throughout your career. No matter what type of business you start, change, or grow, whatever type of product or service you're offering, this content can be used.

This isn't your standard Marketing 101.

I'm taking it to a whole new level and will be sharing many ideas to inspire you and show you how to create magnetic content and attract clients with ease and grace.

Mindset: You're always marketing yourself in life. No matter what you do, you are always marketing. By giving yourself the advantage of understanding that concept, you will acquire a mindset and skill that you will have for life.

Direct Marketing is exactly what it says — you are connecting directly to your prospects, talking to them personally in copy.

Most businesses fall flat on their faces when it comes to fully optimizing the full value of every contact and customer… missing sales by poor, slow or insufficient follow-up, and not developing first-time buyers into life-long, high value customers. Translation: Money LOST!

The correct mindset is key to creating a sustainable and lucrative marketing plan. I invite you to shift your mindset to one that positions you as the MARKETER of that thing you do – you are no longer _____ *(fill in the blank with your title,)* you are now the MARKETER of that thing you do.

This may take some time to adjust to, but trust me on this. Once you shift gears and become the brilliant marketer that I know you are, you will serve even more people because more people will know about you and will actually relate to you and therefore BUY FROM YOU.

Top Five MUST KNOW Direct Marketing Rules

#1: Use Bold Copy

Call out your BOLD, UNIQUE SELF! BOLD COPY and BOLD PROMISES will get people's attention. Being BOLD is NOT optional in today's market. We are bombarded everywhere with various ads: the Internet, Facebook, email ads and so on. So stand out and BE BOLD.

What if being bold isn't naturally who you are? Easy - have someone who is bold take a look at your marketing to see if it's lacking the required punch to be successful in today's market. If they feel like it needs a little more spice, don't be afraid to take their advice! Boldness is power in the marketing world. If no one notices your marketing, then it's not doing its job.

#2: Always Give an Offer

Assume people need to be shown a road map of where to go and what to do next. Tell them in a BOLD way.

WHERE TO GO to claim your offer. Be direct! Always offer something up to your readers.

#3: Give a Reason to Act Now

You can probably guess that the reason for this is that people are busier than ever and we have many decisions to make every day. You need to get your prospect to sign up with you immediately. To entice the prospect, have a Fast Action Bonus that is given to only a certain number of people who register. You want to give them a reason to act now.

#4: Measure Your Results and Continue to Improve

One of the best advantages of marketing online is that it provides the best ways to track and test your marketing strategies. You have the ability to know very quickly if something's working or if it's not working, and if it's not working, you can quickly discover where the problem is.

#5: Always Follow Up

The gold is in the follow up. The biggest mistake you can make when marketing is to promote a service or product and only mention it once, speak about it once, send out one email, put one ad up. *Statistically, people need to see your marketing message seven to ten times.*

Seven to ten times before they'll make a move to click and go see what you're talking about, before they'll fill out the form, call you, or do anything at all to connect with your business. FOLLOW UP.

I encourage you to print these out and have them hanging nearby to remind you every day how to keep honing your marketing skills.

What Is a Marketing Funnel?

Well, in simple terms a marketing funnel is how people enter into your business. Here's how it works. Initially, you start out with a large crowd of prospects (the big opening of the funnel). First, people will flow into your funnel from a wide variety of places. Some will stay and some will travel through your funnel to become loyal customers who purchase your products or services and some will move on.

Fresh prospects come in at the top and your goal is to get them to be happy customers and go out the bottom. As a marketer of your services it is your job to maximize both the number of people you attract at the top of your funnel as website visitors, and also the number that come out the bottom as customers.

Key areas to measure

There are several key terms to become familiar with:

Website Visitors

A measure of the top of your sales and marketing funnel; these are people who found your site. They need to be converted to leads and then customers. Google analytics is a great free resource to see exactly what's happening behind the scenes of your site.

Leads

This is the measure of the middle of your funnel. These are people who visited your site and did something (usually filled out a form) to identify themselves.

Once website visitors identify themselves and become leads, you can begin the conversation needed to turn them into customers.

Customers

The bottom of your funnel — the goal!

Conversion Rates

A conversion rate is the percentage of people who move from one stage of your funnel to the next. If 2% of your website visitors become leads, your visitor-to-lead conversion rate is 2%.

Benchmarks

Benchmarks are data from peers for any data you track. For example, conversion rate benchmarks allow you to see how your own conversion rates compare to similar businesses.

Content Performance

Each type of content you produce should be tracked independently. You want to see how well each type of content is attracting people to your website, and how frequently specific pieces and types of content are used in the process of converting leads to customers. *Source: http://www.hubspot.com*

Attract and Retain

So just how do you attract and retain all those potential customers? Know these three simple strategies.

Where to get found

Online Blogs

Make sure you blog, and that your website and blog are both configured to attract quality prospects to your website from multiple search engines.

BLOG, BLOG, BLOG, then blog some more! You get the idea. If you don't have a blog, GET ONE. 55% of businesses with a blog consistently increase their traffic to their site, which ultimately gives them more prospects to enter their funnel.

Social media

Social media is HUGE. Build your social media campaigns as if you were in a relationship with each individual. You are building your list by being uniquely you online.

Search Engine Optimization

Make sure you are prominently listed on the search engines. It's the first place people look! Find a great SEO person and take an active role in the process.

How To Convert - Lead Nurturing Strategies That Aim To Convert Website Visitors Into Leads And Long-Term Customers.

Call to Action

Tell your prospects exactly what you want them to do: download a report, register for a free webinar, or sign up for a mailing list. Make it urgent by adding a BY WHEN DATE.

Email Marketing

Email marketing (such as an e-zine or newsletter) is a great way to nurture a relationship with your leads. A series of emails focused on useful, relevant content can build trust with a prospect and get them ready to buy.

Make sure that you are "speaking their language." Know your audience and remember: People Buy Results. Make your content relevant and results based!

Website Review

Take a look at your website. Is it clear and easy to use?

What about for someone who knows nothing about your business?

Make sure that what you do is prominently displayed, and more importantly, how they can become a customer. Once the customer has decided to utilize your service or product, make sure they can easily take the final steps to buy.

Take a minute to write down any other thoughts as you review your website.

Learn How To Increase Traffic to Your Website.

In order to get more leads, you should consider how many people go to your website and how you can increase that number.

To get you started brainstorming, consider the following ideas:

- Make sure your site is listed on directories and on all the major search engines.
- Your website should be prominently displayed in your advertising.
- Use email marketing.
- Run regular promotions.
- Continually add content to your site (articles, news, etc.).
- Give away free items or run contests.
- Network, network, network!

Those are just some suggestions to get you started – they are by no means the only ways to increase traffic. Be creative!

Now you have a plan to get people to your page, so what's the next step? Keeping them there!

Developing a solid plan to boost your conversion rates and turn those leads into loyal customers is essential to building your business. There are many things you can do to help turn your leads into customers, but most important is just to BOLDLY SHOWCASE YOUR UNIQUE BRAND.

Being bold and proud of your business will ensure that you are MEMORABLE. If you can be memorable for a lead when they're in the first stages of researching what they want, you'll have a better chance that they will come back and buy from you when they've made their decision.

Marketing

This is a bit like your competition section because you'll want to discuss how you will market your business products or services. What makes your business unique?

No matter which method you use to create your business plan, be sure you are answering each of the questions to make it efficient for its purpose.

Whether it's for you or someone else, the ultimate goal of a business plan is to keep you on track and focused and working toward growth. As your business grows, don't forget to update your plan to grow with it as well.

Market & Customers

Consider the following questions in regard to your target market.

- Who are they? Where are they?

- How many are there?

- What do you need to know about them?

- Why do they need your service?

- Is the market growing? Give specifics about growth and your target market's spending habits. Do as much research on your market as you can and put it in this section, including any barriers or hard to overcome issues.

Creating Your Unique Marketing Plan

- What is your vision (possibilities) for the company?

- What is the purpose (YOUR WHY) of creating the company?

- What is the mission of the company (what you want to achieve)?

Business Information

In this section, note information about yourself and your business. Include your name, business name, entity, address, phone number.

Summarize your business objectives on this page. List your goals and how you plan to reach them.

What will you do to create a profit and what tools and resources do you need to help you?

Competition

- Who are my competitors?

- What makes me different than those competitors? What makes me the same as those competitors?

- How am I competing with them? Price, quality, or something else?

- How will my market feel about me compared to my competitors?

- What makes my business unique?

- What is unique about my product?

- What is unique about my delivery?

- What is unique about my service?

- What industry norms does my company bend or break?

- What is unique about my personality?

- What is my story?

- What is unique about my best customers?

- Who qualifies? What makes them qualify?

- What age group are they in?

Are they male or female?

How much money do they make?

What's their job title?

Now you have the foundation built, so let's create some systems for success!

#8: Design Your Unique Signature Series and Create Multiple Streams of Revenue

Discover how to package your services and instantly leverage your business.

I know for a lot of heart inspired business owners it is sometimes difficult to wear the "business hat." But, we all know success doesn't just happen, much like a gourmet dinner doesn't just appear. In order to have the perfect gourmet dinner you must first have all the necessary ingredients in just the exact quantity. Next, you must have the proper cooking utensils, and so on. Owning a financially successful business requires its own set of must-haves and one of those is a **Signature System** that is **YOU-NIQUELY YOU.**

What is a Signature System?

A Signature System is a series of steps designed around your niche that you market to your target audience. It's a series of steps that you take clients through to get the end **result they want**.

In order to effectively state what the results and benefits of your program are, you must start with **knowing what your clients' greatest needs and concerns are.**

Questions to Ask Yourself

- What is my ideal client's greatest challenge? How do I uniquely help them address or resolve that need?

- What are some of my ideal client's other pressing concerns or needs?

- What solutions do I offer for these problems?

- What is the main result or set of results and benefits my client will get by completing your signature system?

- What are the other benefits my client will get?

Creative Steps

Now that you've identified your client's issues and your solutions, you need to list the steps you actually go through when you work with clients. Take a few moments to center yourself and get in touch with Source.

Because I like to learn visually I prefer to see my progress. I do this by literally laying out my process. I have a stack of index cards or sticky notes and I ask myself if I were experiencing my clients issue what I would do first. Then I write it out and lay it down or stick it to my board. Then off of that I ask what's next. I follow this procedure until I have come to a resolution.

Please note – DO NOT get stuck or hung up in your analytical mind and become overly concerned with how the steps are laid out initially. Once you have them out written down, you will go back and review the order. Trust your inner knowing when aligning the steps. You can always refine them later.

Now is the time to put your steps into modules. It's best to have NO MORE than 7 steps. For each step, chose a clear name and tag which describes what you will do. For example, Module #1 Goal Setting—Creating clear and concise goals to grow your business, or Step #2 Cleansing—Clearing out your pantry of all junk food, etc. So go ahead and order your steps and them give them clear, descriptive names.

Name	Description
1.	
2.	
3.	
4.	
5.	
6.	
7.	
8.	
9.	
10.	

Benefits to Your Client

Finally, and **most importantly**, you are going to name the specific benefit your client will get from completing each of the steps in your signature system. Remember, you are the SOLUTION you clients are looking for. Be clear on RESULTS your system will provide.

Example: Step #1 Goal Setting

Benefits: Clear direction, focused energy, time prioritization.

System Benefits

For each of **your** steps name three benefits your client will get from completing it.

Module #1 _____

Benefits:

a.

b.

c.

Module #2_____

Benefits:

a.

b.

c.

Module#3_____

Benefits:

a.

b.

c.

Module #4_____

Benefits:

a.

b.

c.

Module #5_____

Benefits:

a.

b.

c.

Module #6_____

Benefits:

a.

b.

c.

Module #7_____

Benefits:

a.

b.

c.

I must once again caution you, if you aren't sure who you are talking to it will be very difficult to create a successful signature series. Niching your business really is the first thing you MUST DO to create success. It is critical to your bottom line.

Having a signature system will allow you the freedom to open your business to more people and ultimately make more money doing what you were born to do.

#9: Seven Essential Principles Entrepreneurs Overlook When It Comes to Building Their Businesses and Their Reputations

Whether you are new to owning your own business or you are a seasoned pro, it's time to review and refresh what most of you already know but often times forget – your ability to create your own outcomes in business and in life.

As an entrepreneur who struggled for a lot of years, I decided to write this short and simple guide to help others revive their businesses using simple practical principles that, when **followed habitually, WILL bring you success.**

I encourage you to write on this book – make notes, draw images, express feelings – challenge status quo – **GROW WEALTHY USING THIS GUIDE and YOUR FREE WILL!**

I am going to outline 7 common areas where I have personally experienced growth and success. These specific areas literally have changed the way I do business in every aspect – from getting clients, to retaining clients, to my marketing, to the way I write my copy for all my materials.

1. The Energy of Other People

Who you surround yourself with matters. Negative people will block you energetically. They will block you from achieving your greatest level of success and most will do it unknowingly. Negativity is the result of a particular belief system and most people have a way of being that was handed down to them from their family of origin. Some people unconsciously carry on the tradition of being a drain to all the people they meet, and it's your job to notice it and decide if it disturbs your way of being. If you have ever spent time with an "emotional vampire" you probably won't forget it. As a business owner, keeping your **circle of influence full of clear, positive energy** is key to your success.

The saying "birds of a feather flock together" is especially relevant when you are working on creating a prosperous mindset! **Wealth moves based on responsibility**. If you surround yourself with negative people and you create a victim mentality you will never earn the responsibility to be wealthy. When you play the victim and have self-pity, energetically you are calling more of the same. The greatest and easiest way to attract wealth is when you have a well-developed level of self-respect. Be mindful of victimhood.

Identify some times in your life where you have slipped into being a victim. Who were you surrounded by? What story were you telling yourself?

Take a few moments and think about your closest circle of influence – your immediate family, employees, friends, peers, etc. Next, focus on how being around each of these people makes you feel. Take time and jot down a few feelings that each person brings out in you. Ask yourself who should you be spending more time with and who should you be spending less time with. Once you determine who lifts you up and who brings you down, you need to adjust your mindset accordingly when you are around the negative people. It may even turn out you stop spending time with them or maybe you spend minimal time with them.

2. Your Relationship With Money

This principle is simply about attitude and mindset. Well, it sounds simple, but in reality it may be the hardest principle to follow.

As entrepreneurs, we are all seeking how to transform the world, to fill a void, to live our passion out loud. Our intentions are noble and our hearts are in it, but what we say literally is what sets the stage for our success or lack of it.

Wealth speaks a certain language and travels in a specific circle. I'm not taking about pretentiousness or aloofness. I am talking about your **MONEY STORY – do you speak the language of wealth**?

Your money story (what we discussed in Chapter 1) sets the stage for how you show up in life.

Take time and jot down your money story. What phrases keep coming up for you around money? What beliefs do you hold around money? Are you willing to re-think and re-learn your relationship with money?

3. You Must Sell Your Dreams - Not Your Services Or Products

Sharing your dream with your prospective customers and your existing customers is perfectly ok if done correctly. A lot of entrepreneurs may start out knowing this and some are even operating from this perspective, but as time goes on and fears set in, the idea can get lost.

When you are searching for customers, serving customers and communicating with customers, it's extremely important **to start with the customer experience** and work backward to achieve your entrepreneurial goals.

Entrepreneurs are great at communicating their visions, and many have superior skills when it comes to enticing the prospective client, however sometimes they can get carried away and forget exactly what brought the customer to them. The **ONLY** reason a customer will come to you and more importantly stay with you is because

YOU ARE THE SOLUTION TO A PROBLEM THEY ARE EXPERIENCING – even if the problem is not yet conscious to them.

There is a certain finesse all entrepreneurs must master and that is the **art of storytelling**. One of the greatest storytelling entrepreneurs of all time was Steve Jobs. Whenever he spoke he did it with such possibility and passion we couldn't help but be mesmerized and want to use what he had to solve our problem.

He would tell stories that made us care so much we would walk away being believers even if we didn't enter believing in what he was offering. He captivated audiences using his dreams – and the way he did that was to **MAKE US CARE!** He made us feel like he only dreamed about our needs and what would make our lives better. And, by doing so he created a very successful business for himself! ALWAYS BE AUTHENTIC!

Take a few moments and think about your approach to building your business. How are you showing up to your prospective customers and your existing customers? Take time and ask your customers how you **MAKE THEM FEEL** and **ALWAYS COMMUNICATE TO THEM HOW THEY AFFECT YOU!** Share from your heart – share your dream in way that inspires your prospects to want and need it too. You are building a relationship. Your existing customers are your gold mine; treat them as such!

4. Brand Yourself the Expert

You must walk your talk if you are going to be perceived as the expert in your field. Personal branding is a term that has a lot of buzz around it. When you think about a personal brand think Donald Trump (the granddaddy of all brands), Hugh Heffner, Madonna and the queen, Oprah. These are all extremely wealthy people who have found wealth by **KNOWING WHO THEY ARE**. Their secret is they became the expert on themselves and figured out how to sell it. By simply embracing what matters to them and embracing their values they are positioned as experts in their fields. There are a lot of other components involved, but knowing who you are is foundational.

You may not become the expert featured on the cover of Time Magazine but that does not mean you will not be revered in your industry as the go-to expert.

Personal Branding is simply a way of clarifying and communicating what makes you different and special – and using those qualities to guide your business. It's about understanding and embracing your you- niqueness – your strengths, values, and passions – and using them to distinguish yourself from the competition.

When you know who you are and you are comfortable with whom you are, people are instantly drawn to you and WANT to do business with you! They WILL find YOU!

The world in which we live and do business in has changed. Look at any form of news and you will hear the same thing over and over – we have a soft economy, and people are holding off on spending. Not to mention there are lots of businesses competing for our hard earned dollars. What that translates to is this – **YOU HAD BETTER BE YOU-NIQUE** in your approach to gain new clients and to keep existing clients. **Your you-niqueness is defined in part by the value you provide as well as other critical components.**

The way to begin to define your brand is to identify your values. What are you built on? Next, define what you are passionate about. Lastly, what comes natural to you? Who are you first thing in the morning? What can you not live without?

Know your brand and you will gain expert status!

---

5. Making the Sale Is THE BEGINNING of the Relationship, Not the Result.

In order to attain and maintain #1 in your customer's eyes, you must always put nurturing the relationship first. Assuming you have a committed customer just because they bought once or twice from you is a huge mistake. It is your job to constantly be reaching out to them. It is your job to build a solid relationship based on their needs and wants. **YOU MUST KNOW YOUR CUSTOMER BETTER THAN THEY KNOW THEMSELVES.**

Every interaction we have with people is a relationship. Different relationships require different kinds of attention. You cannot simply assume your customers will love you – you must put your whole heart and soul into the connection.

There is an adjustment period for all relationships and the one you have with your customer is no different. If it is a brand new relationship and you are still in the honeymoon phase, it's all hearts and flowers, constant "touches" via e-zine and special offers. BUT, if it's an older relationship, are you certain the foundation is strong enough to weather the reality of who each of you is?

A critical component to the success of your business is in knowing precisely when and how to upsell to your customers. Once you establish contact with your prospects there is a continuum they will automatically go through. At first they are casually interested, next they are connected, perhaps via products or services, and finally they are committed; they are loyal and more invested emotionally and financially with you and what you offer.

As the continuum evolves it's your job to "touch" them in exactly the right way.

Reaching out just to reach out is never an option. You must have relevant information to prove you have a valid reason for connecting. You must establish a plan.

By putting your customers' needs first, all your efforts must be focused on providing the **RESULTS** your customers are looking for. People buy results to problems they are experiencing. In order to keep the love relationships thriving with your customers you must routinely evaluate the message that you are sending out by asking your clients specifically how satisfied they are with you and your services.

Each person's degree of satisfaction is relative to the problem they are experiencing and the effectiveness of the results you are providing. The ONLY way to continue the relationship is to feed their needs.

To build a strong relationship there are a few MUST DO's:

- Follow the vision of your business.

- Stay true to your brand in EVERYTHING you say.

- Always focus on the RESULTS when communicating with your clients about the issues they're facing.

6. See What's Missing

A sure fire way to position yourself as the go-to expert is to KNOW your target audience and find a way to fill a gap that has yet to be filled by competitors. The gap is the difference between a client choosing you or someone else in your industry. You job is to step up and into the gap to fill the empty market space!

You can do this very simply by first knowing your strength (i.e. your niche) and secondly, by knowing your customers, and then finally by researching what solutions already exist. Once you've done the work your job is to think out of the box, use your intuition and create your place in the market. When creating your position, you want to be mindful of the customers' needs as well as exceeding their expectations. Remember, value is perceived by the customer, and in order to be perceived as valuable, you have to think like they do!

Know Your Customers!

A great example of thinking out of the box is the dentist that specializes in cosmetic dentistry. We all know the market is saturated when it comes to dentists, so one way to differentiate himself is to give the patient the red carpet treatment – pamper the patients with hand and foot massages, paraffin hand wax treatments and lattes while they wait. You get the picture. This dentist is meeting their needs and going above and beyond to walk his patients through the continuum.

7. Passion

Passion is absolutely necessary when building your business. But do not get caught up in focusing only on your passion. In order to make practical business decisions, your thought process should look something like this – **market, market demand, purpose, passion and money**. When identifying your market, search for an underserved market that can afford you. This is the practical aspect on which to build your business.

Passion alone does not bring wealth. You do not simply think passionately about wanting more money and suddenly there is a bucket of money on your stoop – you must **put inspired action and intellect behind the passion.** When you marry all three you have the golden ticket to a prosperous business.

As I said earlier, I have 5 years of being an entrepreneur under my belt. I wish I could tell you it was all roses and sunshine, BUT the truth is it sucked getting to the level of success I am at. I struggled miserably for years. I lost thousands of dollars, alienated people and went through a terrible period of self-loathing.

However, I am here to tell you that I would do it all over again. Of course, knowing what I know now, it would be a cake walk! Well, I can't go back, but what I can do is teach all who are drawn to me my formula for success and save them some pain and loss of time. I define success as having all the free time I want, a flexible schedule, the ability to work from anywhere in the world, and an income that supports the lifestyle I choose to live.

In closing, always remember . . .

Since the beginning of time running a business has changed significantly but one thing has remained the same - relationships. People must feel something before they give you their hard earned money and the only way to get people to feel is to be relatable.

Your job as a business owner requires you to wear many hats and become the expert in a very short amount of time. The competition is fiercer than ever and without the right mindset and tools you can quickly become obscure in an overcrowded market place. My hope is that this book will help you to stand out and will continue to be useful to you as you grow your business and your life for years to come. The principles are time tested and guarantee success when coupled with willingness, and inspired action.

Happy Growing!

Veronica

www.ingramcontent.com/pod-product-compliance
Lightning Source LLC
Chambersburg PA
CBHW051333170526
45166CB00002B/800

* 9 7 8 1 4 9 2 2 6 6 0 6 8 *